NO MORE PEANUTS BOOK 1: HOW TO GET YOUR EMPLOYER TO GIVE YOU A RAISE

No More Peanuts Book 1: How to Get Your Employer to Give You a Raise

Walter the Educator

Silent King Books
A WhichHead Entertainment Imprint

Copyright © 2024 by Walter the Educator

All rights reserved. No part of this book may be reproduced in any manner whatsoever without written permission except in the case of brief quotations embodied in critical articles and reviews.

First Printing, 2024

Disclaimer

The author and publisher offer this information without warranties expressed or implied. No matter the grounds, neither the author nor the publisher will be accountable for any losses, injuries, or other damages caused by the reader's use of this book. Your use of this book acknowledges an understanding and acceptance of this disclaimer.

No More Peanuts Book 1: How to Get Your Employer to Give You a Raise is a little problem-solver book by Walter the Educator that belongs to the Little Problem Solver Books Series. Collect them all and more books at WaltertheEducator.com

LITTLE PROBLEM SOLVER BOOKS

INTRO

Securing a raise is an essential milestone in any professional career, reflecting not just financial gain but also recognition of your value within an organization. However, asking for a raise can be an intimidating and complex process. Successfully navigating this terrain requires preparation, strategy, and the ability to communicate your worth effectively. This little book explores in depth how to approach the process of getting your employer to give you a raise, offering practical steps, psychological insights, and actionable advice to increase your chances of success.

Understanding the Foundations: Why Employers Give Raises

Before making a case for a raise, it's crucial to understand the common factors that drive employers to offer increased compensation. These include:

1. **Market Adjustments**: Employers often provide raises to align salaries with industry standards and remain competitive in attracting and retaining talent.

2. **Merit and Performance**: Exceptional job performance and contributions to the company's goals often justify a raise.

For where two or three
are gathered together in my name,
there am I in the midst of them
- Matthew 18:20

Reiterate
THIS PHRASE
I Will Get a Raise
from my Employer

FREE

DOWNLOAD AND ACCESS THE HIT SONG
"NO MORE PEANUTS"
WaltertheEducator.com/NoMorePeanuts.html

3. **Cost of Living Adjustments**: Inflation and rising living costs can lead to periodic salary increases to maintain employee purchasing power.

For where two or three
are gathered together in my name,
there am I in the midst of them
- Matthew 18:20

Reiterate
THIS PHRASE
I Will Get a Raise
from my Employer

FREE

DOWNLOAD AND ACCESS THE HIT SONG
"NO MORE PEANUTS"
WaltertheEducator.com/NoMorePeanuts.html

4. **Retention**: High-performing employees are valuable, and raises can be a tool to retain them and avoid turnover costs.

For where two or three
are gathered together in my name,
there am I in the midst of them
- Matthew 18:20

Reiterate
THIS PHRASE
I Will Get a Raise
from my Employer

FREE

DOWNLOAD AND ACCESS THE HIT SONG
"NO MORE PEANUTS"
WaltertheEducator.com/NoMorePeanuts.html

5. **Role Expansion**: Taking on additional responsibilities or stepping into a leadership role can warrant a salary increase.

For where two or three
are gathered together in my name,
there am I in the midst of them
- Matthew 18:20

Reiterate
THIS PHRASE
I Will Get a Raise
from my Employer

FREE

DOWNLOAD AND ACCESS THE HIT SONG
"NO MORE PEANUTS"
WaltertheEducator.com/NoMorePeanuts.html

Understanding these motivations allows you to frame your request in a way that aligns with your employer's interests and organizational goals.

For where two or three
are gathered together in my name,
there am I in the midst of them
- Matthew 18:20

Reiterate
THIS PHRASE
I Will Get a Raise
from my Employer

FREE

DOWNLOAD AND ACCESS THE HIT SONG
"NO MORE PEANUTS"
WaltertheEducator.com/NoMorePeanuts.html

Preparing for the Raise Discussion

Preparation is key when asking for a raise. A successful negotiation begins long before the actual conversation. Here's how to lay the groundwork:

For where two or three
are gathered together in my name,
there am I in the midst of them
- Matthew 18:20

Reiterate
THIS PHRASE
I Will Get a Raise
from my Employer

FREE

DOWNLOAD AND ACCESS THE HIT SONG
"NO MORE PEANUTS"
WaltertheEducator.com/NoMorePeanuts.html

1. Research Industry Standards

- Use platforms like Glassdoor, Payscale, or LinkedIn Salary Insights to determine the average pay for your role, industry, and geographic location.
- Consider factors like years of experience, skills, certifications, and job responsibilities to pinpoint your market value.

For where two or three
are gathered together in my name,
there am I in the midst of them
- Matthew 18:20

Reiterate
THIS PHRASE
I Will Get a Raise
from my Employer

FREE

DOWNLOAD AND ACCESS THE HIT SONG
"NO MORE PEANUTS"
WaltertheEducator.com/NoMorePeanuts.html

2. Document Your Achievements

- Maintain a detailed record of your accomplishments, including quantifiable results such as increased revenue, cost savings, or successful project completions.
- Highlight instances where you exceeded expectations, solved significant problems, or contributed to team success.

For where two or three
are gathered together in my name,
there am I in the midst of them
- Matthew 18:20

Reiterate
THIS PHRASE
I Will Get a Raise
from my Employer

FREE

DOWNLOAD AND ACCESS THE HIT SONG
"NO MORE PEANUTS"
WaltertheEducator.com/NoMorePeanuts.html

3. Understand Company Financial Health

- Analyze your organization's financial standing by reviewing annual reports, profit margins, or recent news about budget cuts or expansions.
- Tailor your timing based on whether the company is experiencing growth or constraints.

For where two or three
are gathered together in my name,
there am I in the midst of them
- Matthew 18:20

Reiterate
THIS PHRASE
I Will Get a Raise
from my Employer

FREE

DOWNLOAD AND ACCESS THE HIT SONG
"NO MORE PEANUTS"
WaltertheEducator.com/NoMorePeanuts.html

4. Know the Timing

- Timing plays a critical role in the success of a raise request. Choose moments like annual reviews, after a successful project completion, or during budget planning periods to make your case.

For where two or three
are gathered together in my name,
there am I in the midst of them
- Matthew 18:20

Reiterate
THIS PHRASE
I Will Get a Raise
from my Employer

FREE

DOWNLOAD AND ACCESS THE HIT SONG
"NO MORE PEANUTS"
WaltertheEducator.com/NoMorePeanuts.html

Crafting a Strong Argument

Your ability to articulate your value to the organization is paramount. A compelling case combines logic, data, and confidence.

For where two or three
are gathered together in my name,
there am I in the midst of them
- Matthew 18:20

Reiterate
THIS PHRASE
I Will Get a Raise
from my Employer

FREE

DOWNLOAD AND ACCESS THE HIT SONG
"NO MORE PEANUTS"
WaltertheEducator.com/NoMorePeanuts.html

1. Emphasize Your Value

- Focus on how your skills, work ethic, and contributions directly impact the company's bottom line or key objectives.
- Use specific examples such as "Implemented a new CRM system, increasing efficiency by 25%."

For where two or three
are gathered together in my name,
there am I in the midst of them
- Matthew 18:20

Reiterate
THIS PHRASE
I Will Get a Raise
from my Employer

FREE

DOWNLOAD AND ACCESS THE HIT SONG
"NO MORE PEANUTS"
WaltertheEducator.com/NoMorePeanuts.html

2. Address Future Potential

- Highlight not only past achievements but also your plans for future contributions, including taking on additional responsibilities or expanding your skill set.
- Discuss long-term goals that align with the company's vision.

For where two or three
are gathered together in my name,
there am I in the midst of them
- Matthew 18:20

Reiterate
THIS PHRASE
I Will Get a Raise
from my Employer

FREE

DOWNLOAD AND ACCESS THE HIT SONG
"NO MORE PEANUTS"
WaltertheEducator.com/NoMorePeanuts.html

3. Practice Your Pitch

- Rehearse your request with a trusted friend or mentor to refine your delivery and anticipate possible objections.
- Use assertive, positive language, avoiding hesitations or phrases that undermine your confidence (e.g., "I was wondering if…").

For where two or three
are gathered together in my name,
there am I in the midst of them
- Matthew 18:20

Reiterate
THIS PHRASE
I Will Get a Raise
from my Employer

FREE

DOWNLOAD AND ACCESS THE HIT SONG
"NO MORE PEANUTS"
WaltertheEducator.com/NoMorePeanuts.html

Navigating the Conversation

Once prepared, the actual conversation is where your preparation is put to the test. Follow these strategies to ensure a productive discussion:

For where two or three
are gathered together in my name,
there am I in the midst of them
- Matthew 18:20

Reiterate
THIS PHRASE
I Will Get a Raise
from my Employer

FREE

DOWNLOAD AND ACCESS THE HIT SONG
"NO MORE PEANUTS"
WaltertheEducator.com/NoMorePeanuts.html

1. Set Up the Meeting

- Request a formal meeting with your manager, specifying that you'd like to discuss your performance and future within the company.
- Avoid catching your manager off guard by raising the topic informally or during unrelated discussions.

For where two or three
are gathered together in my name,
there am I in the midst of them
- Matthew 18:20

Reiterate
THIS PHRASE
I Will Get a Raise
from my Employer

FREE

DOWNLOAD AND ACCESS THE HIT SONG
"NO MORE PEANUTS"
WaltertheEducator.com/NoMorePeanuts.html

2. Start with Gratitude

- Begin the conversation by expressing appreciation for the opportunities and support you've received. This sets a positive tone and demonstrates respect.

For where two or three
are gathered together in my name,
there am I in the midst of them
- Matthew 18:20

Reiterate
THIS PHRASE
I Will Get a Raise
from my Employer

FREE

DOWNLOAD AND ACCESS THE HIT SONG
"NO MORE PEANUTS"
WaltertheEducator.com/NoMorePeanuts.html

3. Present Your Case Clearly

- Use a structured approach to outline your request, starting with your achievements, followed by market data, and concluding with your desired salary range.
  - Example: "Over the past year, I've increased sales by 15%, led the successful rollout of [specific project], and taken on additional responsibilities. Based on my research, the market rate for similar roles is $X to $Y. I'd like to discuss adjusting my salary to reflect this."

For where two or three
are gathered together in my name,
there am I in the midst of them
- Matthew 18:20

Reiterate THIS PHRASE I Will Get a Raise from my Employer

FREE

DOWNLOAD AND ACCESS THE HIT SONG
"NO MORE PEANUTS"
WaltertheEducator.com/NoMorePeanuts.html

4. Be Open to Negotiation

- If your employer cannot meet your exact request, discuss alternative forms of compensation such as bonuses, additional benefits, or professional development opportunities.
- Stay flexible and willing to find a mutually beneficial solution.

For where two or three
are gathered together in my name,
there am I in the midst of them
- Matthew 18:20

Reiterate THIS PHRASE I Will Get a Raise from my Employer

FREE

DOWNLOAD AND ACCESS THE HIT SONG
"NO MORE PEANUTS"
WaltertheEducator.com/NoMorePeanuts.html

Handling Objections and Rejections

Not every raise request will be successful, but how you handle rejection can shape future opportunities.

For where two or three
are gathered together in my name,
there am I in the midst of them
- Matthew 18:20

Reiterate
THIS PHRASE
I Will Get a Raise
from my Employer

FREE

DOWNLOAD AND ACCESS THE HIT SONG
"NO MORE PEANUTS"
WaltertheEducator.com/NoMorePeanuts.html

1. Stay Professional

- Remain calm and respectful, regardless of the outcome. Negative reactions can harm your professional reputation.
  - Thank your employer for their time and feedback, demonstrating maturity and composure.

For where two or three
are gathered together in my name,
there am I in the midst of them
- Matthew 18:20

Reiterate
THIS PHRASE
I Will Get a Raise
from my Employer

FREE

DOWNLOAD AND ACCESS THE HIT SONG
"NO MORE PEANUTS"
WaltertheEducator.com/NoMorePeanuts.html

2. Seek Constructive Feedback

- Ask for specific reasons why your request was denied and what steps you can take to position yourself for a raise in the future.
- Example: "I understand the timing might not be right. Could you share areas where I could improve or additional responsibilities I could take on to justify a raise in the coming months?"

For where two or three
are gathered together in my name,
there am I in the midst of them
- Matthew 18:20

Reiterate
THIS PHRASE
I Will Get a Raise
from my Employer

FREE

DOWNLOAD AND ACCESS THE HIT SONG
"NO MORE PEANUTS"
WaltertheEducator.com/NoMorePeanuts.html

3. Create a Follow-Up Plan

- Establish a timeline for revisiting the conversation, such as six months or after achieving agreed-upon milestones.
- Set clear goals and work diligently to meet or exceed expectations.

For where two or three
are gathered together in my name,
there am I in the midst of them
- Matthew 18:20

Reiterate
THIS PHRASE
I Will Get a Raise
from my Employer

FREE

DOWNLOAD AND ACCESS THE HIT SONG
"NO MORE PEANUTS"
WaltertheEducator.com/NoMorePeanuts.html

Enhancing Long-Term Salary Growth

While a single raise can be impactful, developing habits and strategies to ensure long-term salary growth is equally important.

For where two or three
are gathered together in my name,
there am I in the midst of them
- Matthew 18:20

Reiterate
THIS PHRASE
I Will Get a Raise
from my Employer

FREE

DOWNLOAD AND ACCESS THE HIT SONG
"NO MORE PEANUTS"
WaltertheEducator.com/NoMorePeanuts.html

1. Invest in Continuous Learning

- Stay updated on industry trends, acquire new certifications, and develop in-demand skills to enhance your marketability.
- Pursue opportunities to attend workshops, conferences, or courses that add value to your role.

For where two or three
are gathered together in my name,
there am I in the midst of them
- Matthew 18:20

Reiterate
THIS PHRASE
I Will Get a Raise
from my Employer

FREE

DOWNLOAD AND ACCESS THE HIT SONG
"NO MORE PEANUTS"
WaltertheEducator.com/NoMorePeanuts.html

2. Cultivate a Strong Network

- Build relationships with colleagues, industry professionals, and mentors who can advocate for you and provide guidance.
- A robust network can open doors to new opportunities and help validate your worth in the marketplace.

For where two or three
are gathered together in my name,
there am I in the midst of them
- Matthew 18:20

Reiterate
THIS PHRASE
I Will Get a Raise
from my Employer

<u>FREE</u>

DOWNLOAD AND ACCESS THE HIT SONG
"NO MORE PEANUTS"
WaltertheEducator.com/NoMorePeanuts.html

3. Monitor Your Career Progression

- Regularly evaluate whether your current role aligns with your career goals and market value.
  - If your employer consistently undervalues your contributions, consider exploring opportunities with organizations that recognize and reward your worth.

For where two or three
are gathered together in my name,
there am I in the midst of them
- Matthew 18:20

Reiterate THIS PHRASE I Will Get a Raise from my Employer

FREE

DOWNLOAD AND ACCESS THE HIT SONG
"NO MORE PEANUTS"
WaltertheEducator.com/NoMorePeanuts.html

The Psychological Aspect of Asking for a Raise

Understanding human psychology can help you navigate the conversation effectively.

For where two or three
are gathered together in my name,
there am I in the midst of them
- Matthew 18:20

Reiterate
THIS PHRASE
I Will Get a Raise
from my Employer

FREE

DOWNLOAD AND ACCESS THE HIT SONG
"NO MORE PEANUTS"
WaltertheEducator.com/NoMorePeanuts.html

1. Build Rapport

- Establish a positive relationship with your manager through consistent communication and collaboration.
- Demonstrating reliability and alignment with company goals increases the likelihood of support for your request.

For where two or three
are gathered together in my name,
there am I in the midst of them
- Matthew 18:20

Reiterate
THIS PHRASE
I Will Get a Raise
from my Employer

FREE

DOWNLOAD AND ACCESS THE HIT SONG
"NO MORE PEANUTS"
WaltertheEducator.com/NoMorePeanuts.html

2. Use the Power of Reciprocity

- Highlight how your contributions have benefited your team and the organization. People are more inclined to reward those who provide value.

For where two or three
are gathered together in my name,
there am I in the midst of them
- Matthew 18:20

Reiterate
THIS PHRASE
I Will Get a Raise
from my Employer

FREE

DOWNLOAD AND ACCESS THE HIT SONG
"NO MORE PEANUTS"
WaltertheEducator.com/NoMorePeanuts.html

3. Leverage Confidence and Body Language

- Confidence can influence perceptions of your competence and worthiness. Maintain eye contact, speak clearly, and adopt open body language.
- Avoid fidgeting or appearing unsure, as this can undermine your message.

For where two or three
are gathered together in my name,
there am I in the midst of them
- Matthew 18:20

Reiterate
THIS PHRASE
I Will Get a Raise
from my Employer

FREE

DOWNLOAD AND ACCESS THE HIT SONG
"NO MORE PEANUTS"
WaltertheEducator.com/NoMorePeanuts.html

Common Mistakes to Avoid

Several missteps can derail your efforts to secure a raise. Be mindful of these pitfalls:

For where two or three
are gathered together in my name,
there am I in the midst of them
- Matthew 18:20

Reiterate
THIS PHRASE
I Will Get a Raise
from my Employer

FREE

DOWNLOAD AND ACCESS THE HIT SONG
"NO MORE PEANUTS"
WaltertheEducator.com/NoMorePeanuts.html

1. Focusing Solely on Personal Needs

- Avoid framing your request around personal financial struggles. Instead, focus on your professional contributions and market value.

For where two or three
are gathered together in my name,
there am I in the midst of them
- Matthew 18:20

Reiterate
THIS PHRASE
I Will Get a Raise
from my Employer

FREE

DOWNLOAD AND ACCESS THE HIT SONG
"NO MORE PEANUTS"
WaltertheEducator.com/NoMorePeanuts.html

2. Being Unprepared

- Approaching the conversation without research, documentation, or a clear pitch diminishes your credibility.

For where two or three
are gathered together in my name,
there am I in the midst of them
- Matthew 18:20

Reiterate
THIS PHRASE
I Will Get a Raise
from my Employer

FREE

DOWNLOAD AND ACCESS THE HIT SONG
"NO MORE PEANUTS"
WaltertheEducator.com/NoMorePeanuts.html

3. Ultimatums and Threats

- Threatening to leave if a raise is not granted can damage your relationship with your employer and harm your professional reputation.

For where two or three
are gathered together in my name,
there am I in the midst of them
- Matthew 18:20

Reiterate
THIS PHRASE
I Will Get a Raise
from my Employer

FREE

DOWNLOAD AND ACCESS THE HIT SONG
"NO MORE PEANUTS"
WaltertheEducator.com/NoMorePeanuts.html

4. Ignoring Organizational Context

- Requesting a raise during a company downturn or financial instability shows a lack of awareness and consideration.

For where two or three
are gathered together in my name,
there am I in the midst of them
- Matthew 18:20

Reiterate
THIS PHRASE
I Will Get a Raise
from my Employer

FREE

DOWNLOAD AND ACCESS THE HIT SONG
"NO MORE PEANUTS"
WaltertheEducator.com/NoMorePeanuts.html

Conclusion

Securing a raise is a multifaceted process that requires preparation, communication skills, and strategic timing. By understanding employer motivations, presenting a strong case, and navigating the conversation professionally, you can significantly increase your chances of success. Even in cases where your request is denied, staying proactive and committed to growth can pave the way for future opportunities.

Remember, asking for a raise is not just about increasing your salary, it's about advocating for your value, strengthening your career trajectory, and fostering mutual respect within your organization. With persistence and the right approach, you can achieve the financial recognition you deserve.

ABOUT THE CREATOR

Walter the Educator is one of the pseudonyms for Walter Anderson. Formally educated in Chemistry, Business, and Education, he is an educator, an author, a diverse entrepreneur, and he is the son of a disabled war veteran. "Walter the Educator" shares his time between educating and creating. He holds interests and owns several creative projects that entertain, enlighten, enhance, and educate, hoping to inspire and motivate you. Follow, find new works, and stay up to date with Walter the Educator™

at WaltertheEducator.com

www.ingramcontent.com/pod-product-compliance
Lightning Source LLC
LaVergne TN
LVHW021240080526
838199LV00088B/5290